PRAISE FOR *WOMEN & ROOSTERS*

"In *women & roosters*, Fenn Stewart deftly subverts the Canadian colonial wilderness poem, crafting intimate maps of unrequited love that resonate with Faiz Ahmad Faiz's notion that 'the true subject of poetry is the loss of the beloved.' Through precise and polished phrases, she blends eros with politics, offering compelling insights into 'the earth on fire.'"
—ASHER GHAFFAR, author of *Wasps in a Golden Dream Hum a Strange Music*

"'What if prickliness is a form of fidelity?' Fenn Stewart asks in this collection that traces connections between invasive plants, persistent viruses, and a relationship the speaker isn't ready to let go of yet. These poems are luminous, smart company, self-aware, and surprising."
—RIVER HALEN, author of *Dream Rooms*

PRAISE FOR *BETTER NATURE*

Longlisted for the 2018 Gerald Lampert Memorial Award

"With bounding lines that seamlessly blend the archival with the contemporary, *Better Nature* stitches together its source material with precision. The result is pure poetic wit and a timely perspective on the shaping of Canada's landscape."
—*This Magazine*

"By exposing how language continues to build and reinforce colonial structures in Canada, *Better Nature* seeks to tear down those structures."
—*The Goose*

"*Better Nature* positions its writing as parasitic insect, eating away at settler narratives of Canada's natural landscape as uninhabited, undeveloped, and unoccupied."
—*Canadian Literature*

women & roosters

FENN STEWART

Book*hug Press
Toronto 2025

FIRST EDITION

Library and Archives Canada Cataloguing in Publication

Title: women & roosters / Fenn Stewart.
Other titles: women and roosters
Names: Stewart, Fenn, author
Identifiers: Canadiana (print) 2025020603X | Canadiana (ebook) 20250206048
ISBN 9781771669474 (softcover)
ISBN 9781771669481 (EPUB)
Subjects: LCGFT: Autobiographical poetry. | LCGFT: Poetry.
Classification: LCC PS8637.T494453 W66 2025 | DDC C811/.6—dc23

The production of this book was made possible through the generous assistance of the Canada Council for the Arts and the Ontario Arts Council. Book*hug Press also acknowledges the support of the Government of Canada through the Canada Book Fund and the Government of Ontario through the Ontario Book Publishing Tax Credit and the Ontario Book Fund.

Canada Council for the Arts
Conseil des Arts du Canada
Funded by the Government of Canada
Financé par le gouvernement du Canada

ONTARIO ARTS COUNCIL
CONSEIL DES ARTS DE L'ONTARIO
an Ontario government agency
un organisme du gouvernement de l'Ontario

Book*hug Press acknowledges that the land on which we operate is the traditional territory of many nations, including the Mississaugas of the Credit, the Anishnabeg, the Chippewa, the Haudenosaunee, and the Wendat peoples. We recognize the enduring presence of many diverse First Nations, Inuit, and Métis peoples, and are grateful for the opportunity to meet and work on this territory.

Triste est omne animal post coitum,
præter mulierem gallumque

All creatures are sad after sex
except women and roosters

—Aelius Galenus, 129–216 CE

CONTENT WARNING

women & roosters contains references to suicide, self-harm, deaths of animals and people, illness, and injury.

for JSL

the earth's on fire so I go camping

woodsmoke & damp sea air

I know you hate camping, but it's a thing I do

you're gonna have to get used to it

After I've been on the island for a few weeks I get obsessed with Dungeness crabs and spend hours by myself at low tide looking for them in the reflecting water. They halfway dig themselves into the sand like flat and dull-red plates with eyes and brains. The sky and water and air are all the same grey-silver colour. It's May so the crabs are all trying to mate or, y'know, not just trying but pulling it off, and so when I find one it's often actually two, with one on top grasping the other firmly in six places. I pick them up gently with my stainless-steel spaghetti tongs and they stay clasped and look at me with small small eyes with brains behind them. I look back at the pairs of crabs looking at me and then I carefully put them back into the sea and they (still clasped) slide quickly down and sideways underneath some purple slow-floating sea lettuce or whatever it is. I never eat any of them and I tell myself that this is because they're not big enough (six inches across is big enough but only if they're males) or else I tell myself I better not because my cousin (she lives on the island full-time, hasn't eaten meat since she was three and accepted sausages from our grandmother) wouldn't like it. I carry around a thick splinter of cedar that I believe to be six inches long and I measure it against each crab to see how big they are. I check the lines on their pale bottom shells to see if they're maybe full of eggs (if they are, you can't eat them). But really, could I turn them upside down and, with all their small legs waving at me, strike heavily across their midline with an axe, like you're supposed to do, then pull the two sets of legs in half so all the guts fall out into a bucket, leaving just the pale meat in the legs and the ribboned cartilaginous bits inside the body-skull?

Walking back up from the beach. On the right-hand side of the road there's a small dead deer in the ditch, which is otherwise filled with daisies. The deer must've got hit by a car and tossed there, or else, having been struck on the road, made its way painfully into the ditch.

Looking at this small dead deer, I think about how in school they made us read Earle Birney's "David," how he falls off a cliff, I think, hiking, he makes his best friend kill him, a mercy killing. I can't remember how he does it, how he does him in—maybe he puts his hand across his mouth and holds his nose closed? Young men in forests, broken bodies (virtuous bodies), the most grievable-est lives, the most glorious-est accidents, the very best of ends.

Later I learned that Earle said he didn't read Pauline Johnson, which I guess is why we didn't read her either; in English class we traced the Northwest Passage with Stan Rogers, seeking one warm line through this land so wild and — thought ourselves like David, brave as a mountain backdrop, noble as a wilderness suicide, inevitable like holidays on European patios.

The next day I'm walking again & somebody's dragged the small dead deer out of the ditch & back onto the road. I don't know who, though—not a raccoon, surely, & there aren't any coyotes here, nor wolves. A cougar, maybe, though wouldn't it have eaten more? & do they scavenge?

Would you scavenge, really, if you looked like that, & screamed like that, & jumped like that from trees onto living bodies & bit into their spines?

& now somebody's driven over the skeleton & the jaw's in pieces

the deer's skull's full of young & unground teeth

I didn't know maggots could run so fast

the vultures' faces reddened by the eyeless deer in daisies

a vulture's such a sour bird

I haven't heard from you in days & don't know why

didn't you say that we'd still talk?

I'm sitting and watching the birds on the thistles, on the thistle-heads

I'm sitting on the thin porch made of two-by-fours looking out over the thistles, which are as tall as me, and at the birds that are eating them

I want to say without you I'm a joint-stool, without you I'm a rude mechanical

without you I close my eyes so slowly like they do in Sligo, but you're not here and nobody's watching me to see how quietly I take it—so it's no use

I want to say I marvel at how sad I am without you:

I marvel at how sad I am without you

sad like a thistle-head entirely eaten by a bird;

no, sadder, like a thistle-head completely left uneaten

sad like a black-and-yellow thistle-eating bird eating thistles without you I'm listing sideways, a bark that's been shaken

without you I'm cross & itching

I liked it better when you hadn't gone away

I liked it better when you were mad

I want to put my foot down but there's nothing there to stand on like a two-by-four that rotted out of the deck my uncle's fixing with leftover bits of cedar gone like a rotten tooth from a head that wants its tooth back gone like a man with a wife gone like the sleeping bag from the back of my dad's car in high school

I'm writing to stop myself from writing you

I should do something useful I should keep myself occupied I should get some hobbies I should take up carving branches or twisting grass

I should cut you out of my life like a saw cuts a circle out of a piece of wood and the circle drops to the floor and there's splinters and a rough edge marking where the circle used to be and you push the bits through with your thumb and then one of the splinters stabs your thumb and a perfect round drop of blood appears

I'll cut you out with a saw

I'll cut out your careful shoelaces, your shoulder-blades, the specific amount taller than me that you are

I should make a book of all the texts I wrote you in my head when I was running and then never sent you, and then I'll make sure nobody ever reads that book

this is the closest that I've ever been to unrequited love

it isn't great

it's actually pretty bad

without you I'm like a three-legged stool without one leg and then without the other one too so just the one leg, not two-dimensional enough to rest like a penny does when you drop it, and it spins for a while, but then it settles down—I can't settle down if I was still writing to you I'd ask: what do you think about labour, & time? & are you absolutely sure that three women at once is too many?

I'd like to write you a book & name it after you (not your real name, something funny like Travis)

And on the first page I'd write sorry, & thanks

It needn't be a very long book

One night a long long time ago I had a dream in which you were played by Geoffrey Rush, and you/Geoffrey Rush told me that you don't love me anymore, and this made it easier for me to understand that you don't love me anymore, even though you don't look anything like Geoffrey Rush—neither Geoffrey Rush right now, nor how he looked thirty years ago. More recently, I had this dream that you cut your hair off and you shaved your beard.

I've had it twice at least.

And in the dream this makes you happy and it makes me sad.

Last night I dreamed my watch's face got smashed on the floor of an elementary school girls' room.

In real life I don't even have a watch.

There's some guy camping in the woods beside me. He is often there. His tarp is orange. He listens to a lot of Metallica. He makes a fire every night and sometimes it's really large even though fires are usually illegal these days because it's almost always a drought (i.e., forest fires like the one that ate Jasper this morning) unless it's an atmospheric river like the one that trapped my dad in Hope for three days with no highways in or out and no electricity either and the river washed the Coquihalla out in like three places at least, in that valley where everything's named after Shakespeare.

I like the rain more than the fires, like by a lot, but that's probably pretty wrong of me.

I don't know this guy's name. I don't really like it when he's here.

Only one dog is howling in the woods now.

I don't know what it's howling at; there aren't any coyotes here, and to get to any wolves you'd have to cross the Sound, and then a small highway, and then a large highway, and then strike out across a very large forest (once Dad and I saw a wolf print on the beach at Pachena Bay and he measured it with his jackknife; you can tell it's not a cougar print because of the shape—you don't see claws when it's a cougar).

Remember how I told you that my brother got lost in that big forest when we were both small, and we couldn't find him for hours and hours, and the park rangers were looking for him and, at least in my memory, even a helicopter was?

Though maybe I made the helicopter up. And I asked Dad if he was scared, and we were standing there on the long long beach with the open ocean to the right of us and the salal and those funny stunted pine trees on the left, and he said no, I'm not scared. And I've never been so sure in my life that he was lying and I was so mad at him for that. I've never ever been so mad, before or since. Did he think I was stupid? I've never been so mad in my whole life. How could he not be scared? If he wasn't scared, he was either lying or not very smart, and I knew he was smart.

But my brother was clever too, even then, even though he was only five, and he had the idea to walk toward the sound of the sea, and so he walked toward it through the forest for many many hours, and then a man with a dog found him on the beach, and we saw them walking toward us from a great distance. And it was wavy all across the sand, like a mirage, it was all wavy and indistinct where their feet met the sand, but he became clearer as they walked toward us. And so we found him, he found us, and he wasn't lost at all.

Yeah, I know I told you this story before—now I'm telling it again.

When I was thirteen I would have looked up what to do about this in a book.

I probably wouldn't have done it, whatever it was, but I'd have looked it up.

Back in the city, East Van, heading west from my mom's, stuck on a side street near Hastings, the kids are hungry, and I'm trying to figure out where to stop and get food, but I keep hitting all these traffic-calmed street barriers and goddamn one-way-only streets and going in circles—or squares rather, one right-hand turn after another—and we're on Triumph St, near the brewery, and out the window I see something moving in a gravel pothole—

I don't say anything, so the kids don't see it—a seagull dispatching a pigeon, which happens sometimes—

The seagull steps back, lifts his head to check out the car as I pass him slowly—

The pigeon's wing angles out and up and then back down—he tries, but it's no use, he can't get up—

The seagull turns back to him, gets him again with his beak—

I just keep driving, and I think, Vancouver's a city of birds

One spring when my daughter was a baby, my brother and I were at the green house with her and we heard an enormous cacophony. We ran to the back porch and I held the screen door open with my left hip, balanced the baby on my right one, and we could see what it was—the crows had got a baby starling, puffy and brown, and they were eating it alive as its parents hurled themselves desperately against the murder, no chance of stopping it whatsoever, their baby shrieked.

I brought my daughter back into the house so she wouldn't see it. My brother came in a minute later and I hugged him. He was a bit shaky.

One time, this was before I got sick, I was running up a hill & heard the earth breathing

it sounded like ten thousand mosquitoes pressed against the screen door trying to eat me, but in a good way

like all around me were ten thousand people, running up the hill with me, the trees stretched generously overhead, & they were giving us all mouth-to-mouth

like that one time with the robins in Toronto, when they all just suddenly appeared around the apartment, singing in surround sound, stationed right outside my many windows, on the thin branches of the Norwegian maples that would flower with those many-fingered pale green flowers in the very early spring, & I think maybe it's always like this, but we just can't tell most of the time

it's something about those times when you're at the edge; in this case, the edge was that a couple weeks before I'd nearly died in the bathtub at four in the morning (the doctor said call 911 if the pain's unbearable but I figured I was bearing it) while my striped grey cat slept nearby, companionably

Remember last year when we were having such a bad time, and we were like, this isn't working, and I was like, what do you want to do about it, and you said, keep talking?

It's very hot today.

Crows die on days like this, especially the baby ones with blue eyes. They get confused, make bad decisions, end up stretched out in the corner of a parking lot, neck turned to the side and wings stuck out hopelessly.

If you come across them early enough and give them water, it can be enough—if they're still well enough to bestir themselves and drink it, turn their head to the side to scoop up water from the cracks in the pavement (you oughtn't to pour it in their throat yourself), shake off the heat, make a good plan, get under the shade of a tree.

But sometimes you're too late and they're beyond that kind of help and they can only look at you, perhaps they can't even see you, can't even remember that water's the kind of help they need.

On days this hot I do things like watch *Sopranos* with the screen door open, wear nothing but underwear, get a new cat by accident.

This summer I'm reading a lot of books that reject the very possibility that I can read them, or the idea that it might matter if I do.

Two Aprils ago it was very hot for that time of year and I was walking in the woods, down to the beach. I called you, but I can't remember why—just because I wanted to talk to you, I guess. There was something we were supposed to be talking about, some kind of useful practical thing, something we were writing, or something we wanted to try and figure out. I can't remember what. And it was just an excuse anyway. I walked into the woods and then when I came to the right place I stepped out carefully sideways along a downed alder two-thirds submerged in the temporary pond (it dries up every summer). We called it the Swamp of Sorrows when I was a kid. I edged myself sideways carefully along the log, still talking to you, and then sat slowly on my heels and sent you pictures of the skunk cabbage. (I have to remember to look up who it is that digs up and eats skunk cabbage roots, like I've seen along the path on the West Coast Trail—maybe a bear? Is it medicinal?) The skunk cabbage was blooming. You weren't sure if you'd ever seen it before. You told me you didn't really do a lot of hiking or camping when you were a kid. This was before we'd started arguing about camping so I just thought (but didn't say, which was smart—you would have hated it if I had said it aloud), oh that's too bad, and I also thought (but very cleverly also didn't say) about how all the time you were playing soccer you must have been on very short, very green grass with no wisdom, no humility, and no bugs whatsoever or maybe even that new kind of plastic grass that had almost definitely been invented by the time you were in elementary school.

After a while I left the swamp and crossed the road near the golf course where, two Aprils and one summer later, a man my age from Surrey (I almost said a young man) would be shot to death in the parking lot, at almost the exact same time I was riding past with the kids on bikes on the way to school, right next to the piles of logs we take in the winter for my mom's fireplace when the trees crash down on the golf course in the windstorms, and they buck them up with chainsaws, and leave them in the corner of the parking lot with a big sign saying FREE FIREWOOD.

Anyway, back to April, all this time we kept talking on the phone, and I kept texting you these pictures of everything interesting I saw, like bleeding hearts, and salmonberry flowers that were blooming (though I think normally they should be way later than the bleeding hearts, but spring is weird now with this new weather), and the bud of a horse chestnut's cluster of leaves, which looks like a green knot, or maybe a tiny glowing fist covered in golden hairs.

And the whole time we're talking you're texting back about the pictures—you send me an album cover you like, with a picture of an owl and bleeding hearts on it—but in our conversation on the phone we never mention any of the pictures, so it's like two conversations at once, one with eyes and one with ears, until I find this little plant with juicy leaves and flowers that are white with neat little purple candy stripes like someone might wear on her uniform to sell ice cream at Brighton-on-Sea. We stop and look it up—it's called Siberian lettuce, or miner's lettuce. I've never heard of it, and I don't remember ever seeing it, which is rare for me, in these woods especially.

I read once that there's something called "plant blindness"—which isn't a good name for it—it means when people can't tell one plant from another, or don't know what plants do, or what to do with them. When I heard of this term I thought, none of the women in my family have this thing. Maybe one. No. None of us: we know our mugwort from our creeping

Charlie. Actually, I don't know what mugwort is. I know liverwort, but not mug. What does the "wort" mean? I'll look it up, I must remember to look it up. My grandmother will know.

Ok I looked it up. Turns out it's invasive, can maybe cause abortions, and was sometimes used to flavour beer—you ought not to boil it up and spray it on your garden, though, 'cause while it kills the bugs, it kills your veggies, too.

About a month later (still a whole year before I got sick), I was running up this same exact hill—(I used to run up this hill all the time, but I can't do it anymore), and I said to you, "Isn't there a risk, if we just carry on like this?" And you shrugged and said, "Probably, yeah. But it's a risk worth taking," and I was pleased all over like a happy dog, but I also knew that you had no idea what that meant, what it would mean. And you still don't, really.

I learned (from T'uy't'tanat-Cease Wyss) that huckleberry bushes are much, much older than you think. It takes like a hundred years for them to get as tall as me, and I'm not tall. When we were kids, there was a family that wouldn't let their kids eat huckleberries. Huckleberries are blue, they said firmly to their children, so those aren't huckleberries. You can't eat them: they're poisonous, because they're red, and they're not huckleberries. They are, though—I've been eating them all my life, and I'm still here.

One morning, like a month after the Siberian lettuce thing, I was sitting in my car outside a pharmacy where I went to get tested for covid, because that was how it was then, and you sent me an article about gardening in the city, specifically about how many immigrant families have been gardening for food in East Van for like the last hundred years or more, and now there's this whole white hipster gardening urban homesteading thing that gets so much more attention.

I answered you, saying something about my grandmother gardening in her backyard, and how she learned back home in London when she was a kid, with the war and cabbages and everything, and the one egg a week that her dad would get to eat because he was a cop, and he would only give his daughters, one at a time, the broken-off top of the egg that his wife had boiled for him.

You write back saying it's pretty funny how you answered me sending you that article by saying something about your grandmother.

I think about this for a while, and of course you're right, and also of course I keep thinking about my grandmother nonetheless, and about how the woods here are so full of the things that my grandmothers and grandfathers brought with themselves from England: English ivy and English holly, the wrong kind of blackberries, those variegated creeping things with little yellow blobby flowers that are basically unkillable, and of course Scotch broom, which is the same.

When I was a kid, my grandmother always pointed out the Scotch broom to me and told me how terrible it is. There's a saying, "Cut broom in bloom," because that stops it reproducing: you need to kill the seeds before they grow up big enough to spill out of the fuzzy pods and make things worse.

The woods here now are all choked up with all these things, as well as smaller things that don't take over quite as well, like bluebells, which I'm always happy to see in the woods, though of course neither of us should be here at all, and it doesn't matter at all what I think about bluebells.

But broom especially is everywhere, tall and stringy and totally unkillable, you can't even barely break its stems because they just bend; even when you take a branch and bend it backwards against itself it's very hard to make it tear right off.

It's all along the edges of the woods, and in spare lots and ghost towns and all the places that have been logged out (so everywhere, basically).

Once in the spare lot near my place (where we found the snake that one time), I cut a ton of it and brought it home as a bouquet. It didn't smell very good—sort of metal and sourish. It was a different paler kind, with smaller, whiter flowers than usual.

You make fun of me for bringing my jackknife everywhere like I think I'm a Boy Scout or something, which obviously I do. I cut off bits of broom to feel virtuous like I'm helping, which obviously I'm not.

Remember on the very first trip we took together when we found that other snake under the mouldy flat piece of plywood? (A genius! The genius of the place! we said and were so happy.)

Driving back on the Malahat, with the sun coming in and burning my left arm, and you beside me, passenger seat way back, relaxing, which made me mad because why do I always have to be the one to drive, and burn my arm, and not lie back and relax? And you said, "If there's ever something we can't talk about," and I interrupted: "Something catastrophic?"

You shrugged. You looked out through your shady window at the rocky walls the government had blasted through to make the highway, and you shrugged. "Something simple," you said.

(Well, I think you shrugged. Maybe you'll read this and you'll say you didn't shrug. But you did, and the lizard in my brain *flinched.*)

"Something simple," you said.

But I heard catastrophic. I heard something small, and catastrophic.

Something pointy, sharp, and catastrophic.

Back in our separate cities on the phone and I'm walking the alleys of East Van drinking radler out of a jar like I'm 18 or something. It gets dark and there's a constellation. I keep looking at it. It doesn't look familiar. A triangle. And then another triangle at the base of it. Offset. In a different direction. I know the bears, the dippers, Orion, Cassiopeia. I don't know this one. It's not familiar. I'm in the middle of a dark field.

I trace a line across the triangles, and then I trace it again, and there at the end of the field, past a row of dark trees someone planted there (lindens, I think, but it's too dark to tell for sure—lindens grow flowers like little fuzzy balls at the end of tiny little sticks, kind of like if you cut jacks up into little pieces and threw them up into the trees and they got stuck and turned pale green).

There's two street lights and a porch light. The three of them make a triangle too, the bottom two lights, on a diagonal, they're slightly offset, they don't match up. I trace them again and they still don't match. Like the stars, but closer. The chemical yellow colour that the street lights are now.

I trace them, shape the gap between the second and the third. They don't match up.

Once we were sitting in the car across the road from my mom's house and we came up with the idea that our conversations (maybe other people's too)—specifically the kind that go on and on and on and stretch out and snarl up and begin again—are like a kind of walking: sometimes we go fast, and other times slow, and then again at other times we go completely still because we have to, and sometimes one of us goes up ahead and stops, and sometimes it's the one behind who stops, and can't go anymore.

I'm thinking of the word *steadfast*: stand still, hold fast, stay right there, stand fast. I think it was in undergrad, reading Freud maybe, I think it was him, he said all of the oldest words mean themselves and their own opposite, like in Latin: *altus, alta, altum*—like altitude, both high and deep.

A nod means yes, I think. And the opposite of a nod? What happened last night.

Sometimes you stop—I don't know where you're walking.

walking, we're in time and out of it
in joint and out of it

our time itself is out of joint

hard to distinguish—like negatives, we don't show up on film.
if we didn't insist on this it would never have happened at all.
we could have gone on forever without happening at all

we trail behind we lag behind we catch up we stop short we
suddenly stop walking

sometimes, I think we're making something

sometimes, I think there are no words for what we've lost—

not lost: just something we can't have

no ceremonies—

(no. can't say ceremonies)

no words, no ceremonies, no words for ceremonies

running down the hill with you it's steep & I'm off-kilter
laughing 'cause any minute now I know I'm gonna fall &
absolutely shred my face on all this gravel, I'm ok with it

running fast behind you in the woods. your pace is steady & mine isn't—I speed up to jump over a fallen tree & you laugh at me, not breaking stride, & say I look like a Nintendo guy powering up

sometimes you're in front & I watch you run, catch up with you, pass you, I'm better on the sprint (I was then, before I got sick)—I imagine

getting what I want & that makes me faster still. I don't know yet that I will get what I want, but then I'll get sick, & I'll never be this fast again

slowed down like a stone moving underground. slowed down like the mole the farm cat killed, perfect drops of blood on its thick fur. I chased the cat away, its useless silver-foil bird collar glinting in the sun

fast like a stone kicked from a hill-hollow skitters downward on a path

fast like the stone of stony monuments. not stony like a stone-like patience. I knew if I ran fast enough I'd make it happen

my problem's always been I'm not devout enough
I don't know how to undergo, I just banshee

but this time I made it happen, after all, I ran so fast we flew right off that cliff when I was thirteen I was into plants, but not so into birds.

camellia, lavender covered in bees, long grasses on the verge,
the bog's dense springy needle floor, labrador tea, spruce
tips we'd mash with our fingers to hide the smell of smoking,
the plastic gallons of B.C. blackberry coolers hidden under
collapsed sword ferns

that time we each smoked a joint and she was the only one
who knew how to inhale. she freaked the fuck out in the
hallway, screaming that her hoodie was choking her, then
tried to hide inside it

the alder roots in speckled leaf shade

when I was thirteen I kept mouldy jars of tinctures like
feverfew and yarrow in the basement where the turtle once
got lost for three months banging his blunt nose against
the wooden wall unceasingly till Dad found him, dusty and
emaciated

we dropped him gently in the tank where his brother
Rhinoceros was waiting. we all watched him sink slowly,
jettisoning dust bunnies, they floated upwards as, his back
feet touching first, he settled, grateful, or unreflective, on the
dim floor

yeah he was fine. he'll live for another thousand years, eyes
the size of dinner plates. he's probably still in that pond in
Central Park. come to think of it I should go say hi

when I was thirteen we spent a lot of time in the woods, and
not just so my mother's friends and informants wouldn't see
us smoking. the forest closest to my house (the same one

where, later, I'd imagine the coyote'd dragged the kitten) was unsatisfactory all 'round. not like "fields are fragrant and woods are green," as it mostly was when I was growing up, but a strange and unfortunate corner of the forest, like the one in *Titus* where the sons set upon Tamora—"ruthless, dreadful" woods—brushy and dense, no sunshine, invasive holly hedges and scrubby nameless things. without even any alder to grow up quick for 80 years and then crash in a windstorm in November, letting the light in, come the next spring

this ruthless woods, it turned out later, was the site not only of the murder that I knew about from the year before (a guy got jealous and killed his ex's new bf with a hammer as he rode his bike home from school) but years before that even, a man with a paper bag on his head attacked two girls. I heard it on the radio. it was that kind of place, you could tell even if you didn't know.

I can't even remember what we were doing there the time we found a nest of old beer bottles, cigarette packs, smushed-up muddy *Playboy* magazines, yes, actual paper printed ones, yes, that was still a thing then.

that poor kitten, by getting himself eaten by a coyote, kicked off a whole winter of self-harm. I think his name was Cosmo after the ghost of a gladiator from a book we loved as kids. I thought that maybe if I asked the kitten to come back by writing in blood (in a journal with thin blue lines, I can see it now), like Jessica drawing foxes with her own blood in math class, straight razor up her sleeve (where did we get them from? I've never even seen a single person use one for its proper use), maybe that would work to bring the kitten back. I thought: a spell, a proper kind of charm—it didn't

I had to explain self-harm to my daughter the other day because she asked a question. I looked up how to do it right. I probably still fucked it up though—no secrets, no shame, the internet said, and I can see the point of that. I can see the look on my dad's face as he sat on the edge of my bed and asked me

but yeah the charm didn't work: Cosmo didn't come back. it was the beginning or middle of some bad times that stretched out for a few years and then got suddenly shockingly better because she shifted—suddenly against all my expectations or history or anything in life I'd been accustomed to, like struck by a lightning bolt or an asteroid—blasted into someone brand-new I couldn't get enough of

she used to sneak in through the basement window late at night. the shock of doubled arms around a waist, some part of my brain, asleep since infancy, shot back to life, electricity skipping across all the days between, back to that summer, bottomlessly in love with someone else's skin

answering the door, once, to her mother, sloshed at 5 a.m., my tshirt inside out and backwards—

but the summer was also the worst because of holidays away. I'd walk miles and miles to a payphone with heavy pockets full of coins, dizzying hit to the veins when she'd answer the phone (even now, I'd rather not remember what it felt like when she didn't), her voice like air after a thousand years of being underwater, like being dropped into a tank after three months of grinding my nose into a dusty basement wall

but I can see now too why grown-ups feel alarmed or trepidatious, knowing what that sort of tidal wave can do to a person, two persons, so small, such an unstoppable force to be faced within two ones so young and generally, then, unsteady

you can see the sort of thing love does to a person, even now steadfast, a fast stone, a firm stone, a warm stone

a stone's sheer grace is terrifying

what can't I carry with me if I come with you?

that grief is here again; not green-sickness, not the kind green
girls have

but it is a kind grief, the kind with something on the other
side of it

this loss thing comes and goes. sharp as a pointy stone
I wouldn't give it up, I wouldn't trade it

I looked the word up once and found out that a scruple is a sharp and pointy stone

I didn't know you that well then, and I thought you scrupulous, too scrupulous. It's funny in retrospect, I guess

I thought you'd walk away, like this, like a stone walking, in thought: like a stone thinking

I thought you wouldn't give me this, I thought you wouldn't ask me this

I thought you'd just go, like this, with a stone in your shoe, thinking,

but I was wrong, and in no time at all you ran as fast as me

I stand up quickly and I walk to you

you've turned, and I can't see your face

(no, that's not right

I've never even seen you turned

I've never even seen you from the back: I wouldn't even know you from the back)

I'll start again:

I stand up quickly and I walk to you

I'll start again:

you know I’ve got no patience (too hard-hearted)

like a monument, like smiling at a monument, through green
and yellow grief

this loss thing comes and goes

it's here again, sharp as a pointy stone

I wouldn't give it up, I wouldn't trade it

steadfast, with this fast grief between us

fast currents—a sound, a deep unbroken grief

steadfast: two or more things connected, or joined together, bound, or restrained;

firmly tied: an alliance, an agreement, a promise: secure, binding

steadfast: to become attached to a whale by striking it with a harpoon

slow grace: like when you hold your breath

make fast here quickly

here still

Having now been sick for many months, I've decided I need help from humble insects. Keep undertaking things I used to do, but now I can't. Tried to go shopping for food: couldn't even make it home. Gave up and sat on a bench with all my bags around me on the ground. Can't get up. Can't get home. Watching the insects and thinking about their insect plans and highways. Of which I'm bereft. Or no. Just never had. Sitting beside a soccer field and the speaker system is fucked, it's just the first three bars of "O Canada" over and over again and it just keeps on, repeating. Some of the grass beside me is cut and some of it is uncut; the heads of the grass are almost purple and there's something else, quite red, in and among it, maybe sorrel? I need help from these humble grasses. A tire churns up a field, tosses a chunk of sod upside down, the rain washes the protective soil clean off the shrivelly roots, they're all exposed and it's just hopeless for the grass, but calmly so, because it's grass; either it all turns out all right, and the grass gets flipped upside down by a crow, or it doesn't. Either it does come back to life, or it doesn't, and it doesn't matter either way, because there's lots more grass everywhere, with lots of insects in it.

What I have to do now is figure out how to live without the things I need. I almost wrote "what you need." Don't have those either, ha. Thinking this is a question that's posed itself to you these last eight months. Maybe longer; maybe nearly all your life. The "O Canada" thing's still happening. I'm not making this up, it's not a metaphor.

My heart hurts, but maybe this doesn't mean anything as I've made it through the first three heart tests so far. So maybe it's just because I'm sad, and not because I'm sick, that my heart hurts. They think so far my heart itself is fine, probably. But they don't know for sure because I got so claustrophobic in the MRI machine I couldn't stop crying and the nurses were like, honey, just get out of here. This isn't a metaphor either—though believe me, I wish all these things didn't keep happening, all these not-metaphors that look like metaphors, so unseemly.

I wonder if it was better when people didn't talk about things. Don't get me wrong, I'm not making the argument, I know the drawbacks. But I'm just wondering. I talk too much.

I wonder why nobody shuts the damn thing off. And every time the one short bit of the song starts up, some answering alarm chips in with two hoots. Each and every time.

It was Blake who taught his wife to read, wasn't it? Before or after he met God on Primrose Hill. Perhaps in the guise of a humble insect or some humble grass.

The air is thick today, like in *Macbeth*, but thick with atmospheric river, not with regicide

I'm thinking now that I'm the guy whose donkey choked to death on a finger; I'm the guy whose sister left him, sailing off across the Irish Sea (in a very good long mustard coat— an *implausibly* good mustard coat, let's be honest. how could you possibly get a coat as good as that on a tiny little island inhabited by one choked-to-death-on-a-finger donkey & three other guys?)

or maybe *you're* that guy—your face when you looked over & your breath drew sharply & you tried again & you couldn't catch it & you looked at me & you looked from left to right & you couldn't look at me—an intolerable feeling, I said. an elephant standing on my chest, you said. an elephant standing on your chest—you said your heart, you felt your heart, you felt your heart would explode

well anyway he's definitely one of us—either me or you—the guy who keeps walking back down those paths lined with walls of unkind stones, who keeps coming back even though he's been told not to, even though he knows about the shears and the cut-off finger

the guy who just can't understand how this could happen, how you could let this happen

once the too-cruel algorithm sent me something to read
about how couples married for decades
cease to focus on one another's skin
and so suddenly touching a foot or
inclining one's head against a shoulder can remind you

of this whole library that nobody else in the entire world has,
this record of your body, your skin, an archive of decades

like that bit at the beginning of *Trapped* with the gloomy
Icelandic music where the glacier is also a dead man's hand,
but not grim

lines in the earth, geological lines, veins, tendons

it isn't true that I'm not sad

How you fold your arms and listen when someone much
older than you is talking
How straight your back is when you walk into the room
How straight your back is when you incline your head to
touch the floor (*matha tekna*, you said, I don't know how to
spell it)
How your eyes look when I can't see the rest of your face
How your arms rest on your knees when you sit cross-legged;
the ring on your finger, the bracelets at your wrist

How you look when you're paying attention to something
else and then you're suddenly paying attention to me

You used to, when you got into the car beside me, pause as if
involuntarily, and close your eyes and press your head against
my shoulder, the top of your head, the way a cat does, with
the blunt part of your head but, unlike a cat, not asking for
anything, just resting, as if not being with me all that time
had cost you, tired you out, it was only bolstered by my
shoulder you could catch your breath

and when leaving you would, without looking back,
stretch your left arm out across the gearshift—grasp my leg
briefly, not asking or suggesting or looking back or saying
anything—leave

When I was a kid I always thought I wanted to be an old lady, that old ladies had the best deal of anybody I knew, because they start out with tea, and then read books all day in the garden, and then they switch to gin at five

I don't even know if I'll ever be that kind of old lady now; seems a bit unlikely

But the point is I don't see how I'm supposed to get through it all, between now and then

I don't see how

the most notable fault of 2022:
that I can rewrite my excuses, my apologies, right?
sitting in a chair, waiting to be called on: who has the right to call on me for this?

who is it that can sit in judgment, decide on me?

I have a timeline; I can adjust it without lying, these things are hard to put a number on

don't think that I left something out; I wouldn't do that to you

though someone might think that I have left something out—
but I can't worry about that now, not now that it's six of one and half a dozen of a real-life problem

not when I scheduled worry for tomorrow and it's always already tomorrow

In the living room with my dad and my brother reciting
Shakespeare in the 90s
I start cleaning up the dishes

My dad admonishes me: You don't start cleaning up the
dishes! You're listening to poetry! You're transfixed, he tells
me. You're transfixed!

I guess I wasn't, though, 'cause I got up, started piling bowls
I can see one of them, the one on top, an unattractive green
and kinda shiny one, we had it for ages

My brother didn't care, he was probably wearing a bathrobe
My brother was always wearing a bathrobe

The worst part of childhood is, I think, the times you have
that feeling that it's all unnecessary

It doesn't have to be like that

There's something better going on somewhere else—why
can't we get there?

Why do we all have to be stuck in whatever it is we're stuck
in?

But then as a grown-up you can see there are things like
laundry and heartbreak that an adult person can't escape
from, and their kids can't therefore escape from either, except
for the times when they can, running outside, screeching,
jolly, climbing trees

Parents, it turns out, aren't omnipotent, can't leapfrog
gravity, can't make perpetual motion machines, can't make
everything fun, can't possibly, possibly not fall in and out of
love, get hangnails, headaches, lose bills in a dusty pile on the
staircase, forget important things, field-trip permission slips,
make bad lunches, cry

all animals except roosters & women

all animals are sad

all animals except roosters and women

ok I'm maybe sad, but I'm living, I'm alive, I have my shapes & forms

I may be, sometimes, very sad

but I'll become my length in time (I've done it before, I can prob'ly do it again)

I'll stretch out to my full length, I'll press myself against a wall

I'll do—and I'll enjoy it too—whatever is discreditable

a living formative

I'll joy in things, I'll be alive, I'll be so scrutable

I'll come before I'm sent for, like I did last time

when I came before anyone asked me to

there's a pond in the woods near my house made from an old quarry. it has quiet ducks and loud bullfrogs and the first salamander found in the city in the last 20 years. my son's afraid of those woods (zombies) but still we go and we sit on the rocks and watch the methane bubble up and wonder what the ducks are finding in the mud. the bullfrogs sound like enormous snapping elastic bands and I somehow never see them, just the splash a second too late

I used to think my biggest problem is, my mettle's too undaunted. coming up with all this life in the first place, wanting to fight those guys on the ferry, imagining that I'm infinite, that I can do it all on my own, school runs and rent and driving everyone to their therapists all over this city, and the city next to us, and the city next to that, and not letting the berries go bad too quickly on the counter, or get squished mysteriously into the car seats

but now I think you maybe get pressed down, over time, worn out—I mean, I have, I am

before, for sure, I'd send Malvolio after you with a ring, embarrass myself—I mean, I did, and it worked, and you sat in my car with your head in your hands like Dave in the song, and you've been there since (I mean, off and on)

and I've never really minded making an ass of myself in public—maybe it's easier for me, never having been legitimate—and yet my letters are speedy, & both my daughter & her inventions thrive

a low centre of gravity, hard to knock over, a bundle of straw, a family of women, workhouse moms, our base, not proper, prospers a funny Communist I knew in Toronto once listed the oldest words that end in -ard and told me how they work: like bastards (those who are base), and cowards (those who are cowed), laggards (lagging), mallards (butch), and wizards (wise)

and see, just like that, gods stand up, after all: on placards, with standards and flags

his banner over me was good; I'm sorry that it's gone

& I dunno now if I ever will become my full length

though at least I'll always have been discreditable

I'll always have come before I was sent for

before anyone asked me

before they asked me to

there was a suicide on the skytrain

someone wrapped some faded wool around a little dying tree

nightjars have eyelashes

they love flat roofs

the city is grey & the trees are a darker grey

every morning, very early, when it's still grey & before you can see Mount Baker on the other side of the river, the train runs past the fork in the path at the edge of the woods

& every single time I think about that day when we met in these woods (we were still on our mission of looking for the oldest tree in the city) & we couldn't find each other & I was wearing those blue shorts that were really too short for sitting in the woods & I got spiky little dead bits of cedar stuck all over the backs of my legs & I tried to brush them off subtly because we didn't know each other that well then but my legs were sticky & the bits stayed on

the closest we ever really got to the big ones was the time we drove through the clearcuts on that windy little logging road & the raven flew ahead of us for miles

One time I asked you, what if prickliness is a form of fidelity?

I got a shirt that says "happy camper" from the giveaway pile,
just to make you mad

look, I think that what we have to acknowledge is

the last however long it's been wasn't just the result of some Herculean effort to reshape the universe

the world has helped us be in the ways we want to be, helped us live how we want to live

it isn't just about reordering things, it's about the things we fall into and move with

a green worm's crawled itself inside the doorframe, the back doorframe, and is carefully surrounding itself with fuzz in the process of turning into something else, so I can't close the door

and every fucking morning that goddamn thrush wakes me up at like 4:30, a Swainson's thrush specifically, you know the one that sounds like an algorithm wrote its song to prove that music is the same as math. I think, if I ever meet a Swainson's thrush, like face to face, I'll fight 'im

there was one summer I was waiting for a baby in my family (not my baby) to be born

that was the only time I ever slept here, in the little green house in the woods in the clearing, all on my very own

I was not afraid, not really

in the afternoon it became terribly hot and still and I poured the sulphurous water from the well all over my head

I ate three peaches and some dried meat from the store

there was a thunderstorm the night I came back home. the baby still not born, but on the way, thunder and lightning, but no rain. I found out later they call it dry lightning, it starts a ton of wildfires in the woods

the night before I'd spent sleeping in my car to be as close as possible (but not too close—that summer we were worried about covid) so I'd slept in the car as close as I could get to the house but a streetlight shone on me treacherously from next door where drunk men spilled out onto a party lawn. they were loud and they were annoying in and of themselves but also a bit worrying because it seemed to be the sort of scene one didn't necessarily wish to get entangled in by accident, by being spotted through a car window, sleeping all alone under a streetlight

nothing happened, but anyway I was tired the next night, getting home. and in the morning there was a message on my phone, the baby had been born

ACKNOWLEDGEMENTS

Most of these poems were written, and take place, on unceded Skwxwú7mesh (Squamish), xʷməθkʷəy̓əm (Musqueam), and səlilwətaɬ (Tsleil-Waututh) territories. The poems in the first part of the book take place on Sla-dai-aich / tay'stay'iĉ (Denman Island), part of the unceded territories of the Pentlach, K'ómoks, Homalco, Klahoose, Qualicum, Shíshálh, Tla'amin, We Wai Kai, and Wei Wai Kum peoples.

These poems include quotations from, and references to, a number of Shakespeare plays, especially *King Lear*, *Titus Andronicus*, and *Twelfth Night*; the song "Sprinter" by Central Cee and Dave; and "Interlude," a poem by Asher Ghaffar, and the *Oxford English Dictionary*.

Thanks to my lovely editor, Sandra Ridley, for her smart and generous work, and for backing me up when I felt wobbly. To Mom, Dad, Nanny, Karen, Kerry, Yeva, Lev, Anton, and Pasha, for many and various things. Double thanks to Reed for the cover rooster. To Haeden for not getting lost. To the Port Moody Wild Cattle Society for keeping me going. To Angie for signing off on the historical bits, and for being there all this time. To Afuwa (and Marci) for sweet potato pies and for reminding me, at a crucial moment, that people change, and that things change, too. To my students and colleagues at Capilano U, for my job which lets me both live and write. To Gus for the support group, Sean for the boundless enthusiasm, and Mat for taking the time to read this, despite your moral reservations about love poetry. To Andrew my mandrew, for making it seem possible. To Evan, for reminding me about literary composites. To Shawn, for all your help. To everyone at Book*hug, for everything that you do. And to Jastej: just thanks, not sorry.

ABOUT THE AUTHOR

PHOTO: ANGIE DUBÉ

FENN STEWART is the author of three chapbooks and the poetry collection, *Better Nature*, which was longlisted for the 2018 Gerald Lampert Memorial Prize. A former editor of *The Capilano Review*, she continues to serve on the magazine's editorial board. Stewart holds a PhD in social and political thought, and teaches literature and writing at Capilano University. She lives with her kids in Vancouver, B.C., on unceded Sḵwx̱wú7mesh (Squamish), xʷməθkʷəy̓əm (Musqueam), and səlilwətaɬ (Tsleil-Waututh) territories.

COLOPHON

Manufactured as the first edition of
women & roosters
in the fall of 2025 by Book*hug Press

Edited for the press by Sandra Ridley
Copy-edited by Stuart Ross
Proofread by Hazel Millar
Cover by Malcolm Sutton
Type + design by Jay Millar
Cover image: Reed Stewart
Printed in Canada

bookhugpress.ca